Early Childhood Education: Taking Stock

Edited by
Philip Gammage
and
Janet Meighan

Education Now Books

Published 1993 by Education Now Publishing Co-operative
P.O.Box 186, Ticknall, Derbyshire DE73 1WF

Copyright © 1993 Education Now Publishing Co-operative

British Cataloguing in Publication Data

Gammage, Philip and Meighan, Janet

Early Childhood Education :
Taking Stock

I. Title

.372.942

ISBN 1 871526 13 2

This book is sold subject to the condition that it shall not, by way of trade or otherwise, be lent, re-sold, hired out, or otherwise circulated without the publisher's prior consent in any form of binding or cover other than that in which it is published and without a similar condition being imposed on the subsequent purchasers.

Design and production: Education Now Books

Printed by Mastaprint, Stapleford, Nottingham

Contents

Introduction
by Philip Gammage and Janet Meighan — i

Why not happiness? Reflections on change and conflict in early childhood education
by Marian Whitehead — 1

Four year-olds in school: cause for concern
by Jenefer Joseph — 10

The professional identity of early years teachers: challenges and constraints
by Iram Siraj-Blatchford — 21

Early childhood education..... Where are we now?
by Rosalind Swann and Philip Gammage — 31

Postscript: Early childhood education: ten points of good practice — 46

Notes on contributors — 47

Early Childhood Education............Taking Stock

Introduction

One of the distressing paradoxes of educational life in Britain of the 1990s is the status and condition of our early years education. Whilst our primary schools are still very much admired throughout the world, appropriate under-fives provision is undoubtedly poor, especially in comparison with the provision elsewhere in Europe. Only some 45% of our three-year-olds are in properly organised nursery schools or classes. Yet the quality of that insufficient provision is often very high and, moreover, admired internationally. One can often discern developmental practice of the highest order. One can find nursery schools or kindergartens that are excellent. The provision, however, is patchy and the current government persists in regarding that mixed and often uneven provision ('guided', that means unplanned, by market forces) as being entirely appropriate. 80% of our four- year- olds have some sort of provision, they claim. Yes, if you add in the fact that the rising fives are in (often) entirely inappropriate primary classes. Yes, if you perceive play-groups and childminders as a thoroughly satisfactory educational equivalent! Yes, if you regard it as responsible of our government to ignore research and professional advice and permit the relatively untrained to have the care and education of many of our nation's children. Yes, if you regard it as satisfactory for the poor and needy to face costly alternatives, or worse, none at all, at the very time when they, that is the single or low-wage-earning parent, are desperate to find work.

The writers in this slim volume are concerned with the current state of early childhood education in England and Wales. (Scotland has a different system and, in some respects, has fared better than the rest of Britain.) They wish to take stock of that mixed provision for our children under the age of eight years or so. They are anxious that nursery and primary school practices fit properly and educationally together. They are concerned with the fact that, years after the intervention of the McMillan sisters, the pioneering work of Lillian de Lissa, and the careful research of Susan Isaacs, we still have an inadequate and adhoc system for our young. It is a volume intended to summarise where we appear to be, perhaps to shake our complacency, to remind all of us that there is ample evidence that good, proper early years education pays the society handsomely. It is a reminder that we appear to have been 'brainwashed' by many of those responsible for educational policy, brainwashed into believing that we can't afford it, or, as bad, brainwashed into believing that current primary practice is responsible for society's ills. As they are beginning to note in the USA (vide the National Education Goals report, 1991), a society which cares about its future cannot afford to take such a short-sighted attitude

Education is an intensely political matter. Early childhood provision may be especially so. Its staff are largely female; and current government proposals appear to downgrade training and, if such proposals succeed, eventually, such staff will have lower status than their other teacher counterparts. What nonsense when ample research evidence now exists to demonstrate that high quality provision not only pays, but depends upon high quality training. What nonsense when even relatively impoverished 'developed' countries are seeking to provide full-scale educational provision for all children of three or more who need it (for example, New Brunswick, Canada; and Portugal)!

Recent visitors from European Community countries have already remarked 'how scandalised' they are by the fact that such little time in existing teacher-training can be devoted to theories of pedagogy or child development. They have commented on our over-reliance on apprenticeship styles of training which laud methods more akin to 'sitting by Nellie'. They have reminded us that, whilst theory is no substitute for practice, practice is also no substitute for theory. A proper balance is required.

Thus, comments on what other countries provide, what some of the research indicates, what some of the implications might be for our youngsters if we continue our haphazard provision, what the implications for the profession are of current policies on teacher education and training; these are all issues which appear in this slim volume.

Marilyn Jager Adams is probably right:

> *"Education is about opportunity and enfranchisement. It is about knowledge, economic potential, self-determination, perspective, and power. Education is inherently political.* **Given full commitment,** *questions of how best to achieve it are issues that belong, not to politics, but to science and pedagogy." (Adams, 1991, p395)*

We doubt both the commitment and understanding of the present policy-makers, with their goals of market-forces and their rhetoric of individual responsibility. We doubt the wisdom of the advice they employ. We doubt that the country can any longer afford to have an inadequate system of early childhood educational provision. It is now almost ninety years since Lillian de Lissa set up her schools for the poor in the Adelaide suburbs. It is now one hundred and twenty years since France provided ecoles maternelles for all its three-year-olds. How much longer must the British wait? What more evidence is necessary? To fudge the issue (as do current initial training proposals, 1993), to delay much longer, when we know how quality can be achieved, is to mortgage the future.

Philip Gammage and Janet Meighan

REFERENCES:

Adams, M.J. (1991) A response by Marilyn Jager Adams, *The Reading Teacher*, 44, 6, pp 386 - 394.

The National Education Goals Report (1991) *Building a Nation of Learners*, Washington, DC, NEGP.

Why not Happiness? Reflections on change and conflict in early childhood education

by Marian Whitehead

A change of tone

Changes in language are usually the first sensitive indicators or radical shifts in a society's attitudes and policies. Nowhere is this more true than in the complex field of education and care provision for young children. An early sign of such changed priorities can be found in the comments made by a government minister some time ago alleging that nursery schools were places where much painting and happiness could be found, but not much learning! This slick language, derived from the ethos of big business, is epitomised by slogans such as 'no pain, no gain' and points towards a strange new world for early childhood professionals. A world far removed from that of care and education in kinder-'gardens'. However, the new shift of attitude and language is not that new, it is deeply rooted in an old tradition of cheap and brutalising schooling in Britain and 'shift for yourself' child-care. Evidence that in England and Wales we are moving once more into an era of 'hard' as opposed to 'soft' control of schools and children (Hartley, 1993) has accumulated steadily since the Education Reform Act (ERA) of 1988 placed control over curriculum content and the manner of its 'delivery' in the hands of the Secretary of State for Education. The various functions and mutations of the so-called advisory bodies such as NCC, SEAC and SCAA are neither here nor there in this argument. The new trend is encapsulated in the 'new' metaphors, most of which are very old indeed, but dusted down for a re-run of the 19th century approach to schooling.

Once again, we find that politicians provide the most helpful and direct linguistic indicators of change. A former education minister recently listed the things which parents or nursery schools must teach children before they start statutory schooling: 'recognition' of days, months, colours and numbers, and the skills of dressing unaided and ordering objects by size. This strange little list contains some useful precursors of mathematics and some cultural niceties, but note the justification for it which is offered:
> *"Instead of trying to give children this background when they get there, schools can then start teaching from the first day. A school is for teaching in. It isn't a Butlin's holiday camp."*

(Sir Rhodes Boyson, TES National Curriculum Update, April 1993, p.4)

What is striking about these comments is the combination of ignorance of how children learn in the early years, their active acquisition of complex cultural, linguistic and mathematical concepts is dismissed as 'background' which can be 'given', with an implied contempt for early years teachers and their professional skills and judgements. This is all focused in a specific metaphorical reference, the Butlin's holiday camp, which is saturated with notions of distanced power, snobbery and controlling and amusing the masses. Yet it is important to be clear that masses are just other people, like you, me and our families and friends (Williams, 1961). The holiday camp metaphor is being used here to suggest the need to impose uniformity, obedience and discipline on other people and their children, while also castigating the idle pleasures of holiday camps. In contrast, my own observations (Whitehead, 1992) of young children on holiday by the sea, although not in a holiday camp, indicate that a high level of intellectual stimulus encountered in early years classrooms is being worked on and developed in relaxed holiday play:

> *"Freed from the need to conform to arbitrary and imposed standards for satisfactory performance in moving sand, laying paths, capsizing air-beds, or locating a hotel room, these children extended their bodies, their minds and their understanding of a range of facts and phenomena, beyond anything that could be demanded in a test."* (Whitehead, op.cit. p.96)

It is not just those who might be said to hold traditional utilitarian views on the purpose of schooling who use the language of stern and joyless control when commenting on early years education. Recent well-motivated 'good' press publicity highlighting the substantial social, personal and economic benefits of quality nursery education, as researched and monitored in the USA (Schweinhart & Weikart, 1993), was couched in terms of 'you get back what you put in' (Daily Mail, 21.4.1993, p.17). Bearing in mind that the receptacle referred to here is a young child, we would do well to feel uneasy about this imagery which evokes nineteenth century banking, or more contemporary medical injections and vitamin supplements, or even violence and abuse. Why is current political and media talk about early childhood and education dominated by alarmingly inappropriate language and metaphors? In order to engage with that question we need to explore some alternative ways of thinking about young children and early years curricula.

Conflicting views of early childhood

The previous comments should have indicated that we are already in a period in which public debate about education is working with a narrow set of definitions. Teaching is frequently assumed to be a simple matter of transmission: teachers tell and do things to pupils. Learning is characterised as at best passive reception and at worst stressful. Children are taken to be empty vessels, unmoulded clay, or recalcitrant recruits to the human race who must be licked into shape and fitted for society. These grimly instrumental views have recently been expanded by some 'afterthoughts' proposing a moral and spiritual dimension to the national curriculum (NCC, 1993). Yet it is hard to see how teachers can possibly function as the required 'models' of morally autonomous persons for the children in their care, when they are themselves deprived by legislation of the personal and professional responsibility to think for themselves and make educational and moral judgements. In this respect, it is interesting that the NCC document focuses on teachers' functions as moral agents in terms of how they dress, use language and put effort into their work! One current moral issue goes unremarked in the official discussions. That involved in the proposed legislation is the formalisation of the status of prospective teachers of children under-eight as less educated, less well paid and less carefully selected and monitored (DFE, 1993a). But worms are beginning to turn vigorously and the challenges from teachers and parents to the prevailing dogma are supported by a wealth of scholarly research and good sense!

> *"The child and psychologist have at least one significant common goal: the understanding of human action. Both are in the business of trying to **interpret, predict** and sometimes even **control** what people do."* (Bennett, 1993, p.1)

There is a long tradition of developmental studies in cognitive and social psychology which shows that very young children, those in the first three years of life as well as in the early years of education (3-8), behave like psychologists, scientists and linguists. This is generally known as the tradition of everyday or folk psychology (Bruner 1990, Bennett 1993), but it is not restricted to childhood. It offers insights into the strategies we all develop for making sense of our lives and experiences. We do not wait to be told about ourselves and the world but, using minimal resources in infancy, set about creating possible scenarios and predicting likely outcomes. Our minds have been described as constructing theories of the world and acting on these mental constructs (Kelly, 163) as if they were scientific hypotheses which give a degree of predictability to the flux of events. Our predictions can, of course, be wrong but the experience of a mismatch leads to the sort of learning in which we modify and fine tune our versions of people and events. This may appear to be taking us a long way from the early years classroom and yet the little child who has clearly classified adults as nice people/naughty people, or family and strangers, has a powerful tool for beginning to discriminate, predict and even control human behaviour. Similarly, the baby can classify and refine to some extent the potentially confusing impact of sensory information encountered on all sides by using broad opposites for sorting experiences, as in 'hot' like coffee or 'cold' like floor tiles. All this very early learning which underpins so much of our later adult thinking and behaviour is clearly bound up with our first human relationships, languages and culture, but it appears to lock on to a mental system which is predisposed to work in terms of contrasting categories, same-again features and story-like predictions.

Current research might say that we all act like psychologists because we have a theory of mind, we act on the assumption that others have minds too, minds which are not empty containers to be filled but complex systems of beliefs and predictive strategies, just like our own. Thus we can see this everyday psychology at work in the young child's complaint, "nobody don't like me" or in the anxious query, "why are you annoyed with me?" Children and adults, it would seem, are complex, non-linear systems (Bruner, 1990, Bruce 1991), not easily programmed or filled in, but rich in highly adaptable cultural and affective strategies for coping with life in communities. Very young children may lack sophistication and experience of the world but there is evidence that they develop remarkable 'expertise' in language, interpersonal communications and the symbolic representation of experiences.

The child as expert

The notion of the child having expertise in the pre-school years challenges the assumptions of traditional schooling and of the current legislation and debate, as outlined in the first part of this chapter. Furthermore, it leads to radically different conceptions of what constitutes an appropriate early years curriculum (Blenkin & Kelly, 1988, EYCG, 1989, 1992). The special expertise of young children can be identified in three areas of understanding: the linguistic, the interpersonal and the representational. Perhaps we might identify our child 'expert' as a remarkable linguist, sociologist and artist!

Children learn their first languages by subtle, sensitive processes which involve tuning in to contexts and situations and making deductions about words, meanings and rules as they are used. These social and linguistic hypotheses are tested out by young language learners in crucial exchanges with important carers, siblings, and even toys and pets. Language is learnt because it keeps children in contact with others, it takes them into a way of life, and it gets things done for them. Sounds shaped on the outgoing air from the lungs bring cuddles, ice-creams and piggy-back rides!

Language is learned in close relationships with important people and the essential pre-verbal foundations of language are laid by the establishment of patterns of mutual attention and pre-linguistic communication between infants and carers. This is not a simple matter of input from the adult only; very young babies initiate and terminate eye-contact and periods of very expressive babbling and smiling. This achievement of joint interest and attention between baby and carer certainly facilitates a focus on naming objects and people and sustaining 'conversations'. It also initiates infants into the subtle social skills of a lifetime, such as, reading faces, interpreting body language and gestures and picking up on tone of voice and the tunes of languages. The deductions which we make about people's states of mind from these readings shape our lives, personalities and relationships, yet we get started on the activity before we can speak.

If young children can be described as expert linguists and sociologists in the years before school, they can also be characterised as artists who handle and shape experience by representing it, in order to understand it better. Grand claims perhaps, but very young children who have just learnt to talk, take the raw material of their daily routines and turn them into narratives in which they mull over the oddities of people and life (Weir, 1962, Nelson, 1989). These particular two-year-olds were talking to themselves in bed before falling asleep, but the stories which children tell themselves soon take centre stage in their daily lives and become a major means of making sense of experience (Wells, 1987). Again, this device for going over, or representing, experience in order to make sense stays with us. We all shape the happenings of the day into a sad or funny story to tell ourselves, or another, when it is all over. This is the great attraction of gossip and stories to dine out on, but young children must work extra hard to fit many puzzling happenings into their limited experiences of the world beyond the home, the immediate community and school. There are curricular implications to be noted here, best expressed by a poet with humour and economy:

6 Marian Whitehead

> *"He knew a lot of time: he knew*
> *Gettinguptime, timeyouwereofftime,*
> *Timetogohometime, TVtime,*
>
> *Timeformykisstime (that was Grantime).*
> *All the important times he knew,*
> *But not half-past two)."*
>   (U.A. Fanthorpe, 1992)

The young child's keen awareness of time as a means of structuring daily social living and ignorance of the conventions of time as dial-reading, illustrate both the problem and the key to an appropriate early years curriculum. New learning must build on what children know and understand already: the more abstract and difficult the concepts, that is, the more remote they are from daily experiences, the more help children will require to anchor them in a known world. This is the art of teaching and it involves far more than 'tricks of the trade' and following national guidelines, it demands hard thinking and knowing children and communities well. But it is important to emphasise that children do not just sit around waiting for others to make sense of things for them, nor are they restricted to representing their experiences through talk and narrative alone. Infants and young children can be observed repeating and going over events, ideas and feelings by means of gestures, whole-body movements, and all the range of activities we call play: pretending, building, acting, making, drawing and painting.

This daily and often under-valued mix of play, language and social skills is the real foundation of cognitive development; its components are more truly described as 'basics' than the usually cited conventions of written language and mathematical notation. An appropriate early years curriculum endeavours to reflect these priorities in a holistic approach to individual children and to knowledge. Implicit in this approach is a belief that children are already on the way to becoming thinkers, readers and writers in their homes and communities. This is well-expressed in the notion of joining a language and literacy club (Smith, 1988), perhaps as new and not very experienced members, but keen players none the less!

Early years educators talk of young children's intellectual development in terms of their 'emerging' as writers and readers and investigative mathematicians and scientists. We could add to this the helpful notion of very young children as real-world geographers and historians who are eager to explore their own sense of place and community, time and change. Such exploring begins in lively physical activity, story-sharing and involvement, the recording of findings comes later and is not restricted to words, numerals and teacher-led versions of experience.

Where are we now?

We are, it would seem, on the cusp of change. Furthermore, the shifts in public language identified at the start of this chapter signal a new agenda which must either dominate, or be resisted. One simple answer to the question, why such a sharp change in language and metaphors about education, is that we are being prepared for a different approach to schooling at all stages. An approach which drops all claims to be influenced by research and knowledge about child development and human thinking, and elevates social requirements above individual quality of life. A stark summary points up the nature of the choice for early years professionals and parents. Either, we defend a holistic curriculum which respects children and presents knowledge as generalised sets of representations which must still be shaped by individual sense-making strategies, strategies rooted in familiar communities and particular ways with words (Heath, 1983). Or, we work obediently with imposed nineteenth-century conceptions of distinct subjects, correctness and social control. At present this battle is focused on the new proposals for English (DFE, 1993b) and the 'control agenda' is transparently clear in the issues of compulsory spoken Standard English dialect, prescribed lists of bits of books, and a methodology for reading teaching which privileges phonics and putting language together in externally controlled sequences. Other curriculum areas show the same influences: history has become dominated once again by the 'facts' of white, male, imperial stories; art and music are increasingly about great people and great works. The utilitarian advantage of this kind of curriculum is that any idiot can follow the instructions and do it - or deliver it! The 'idiot teacher' (Holmes, 1977), narrowly trained on the job and not encouraged to think too deeply, will 'deliver' and not rock the boat of state.

It is clear that in the months and years ahead the realms of developmental psychology and Rousseau-esque romanticism about 'the child' are not going to be strong enough defences (Hartley, 1993). Parents and early years practitioners must face up to the hidden curriculum of the nursery and infant school which operates to control the 'masses' and preserve the status quo for those already in receipt of life's 'goodies'. We must articulate the kind of early years education and society we want. Do we settle for quality early years provision so that we can lower future crime and truancy statistics, or, so that our children can be happy in the present and fulfilled in the future? The difference is not academic hair-splitting, it matters. Parents and professionals must not be afraid to ask, why not happiness now?

REFERENCES:

Bennett, M. (Ed.) (1993) *The Child as Psychologist*,
    Hemel Hempstead, Harvester Wheatsheaf.

Blenkin, G.M. & Kelly, A.V. (Eds.)(1988) *Early Childhood Education: a developmental curriculum*, London, Paul Chapman.

Bruce, T.(1991) *Time to Play in Early Childhood Education*,
    London, Hodder & Stoughton.

Bruner, J.S.(1990) *Acts of Meaning*, Cambridge, Mass., Harvard University Press.

Department for Education (DFE)(1993a)*Draft Circular, The Initial Training of Primary School Teachers: New Criteria for Course Approval*,
    London, Department for Education.

Department for Education (DFE)(1993b)*English for ages 5 to 16, Proposals of the Secretary of State for Education and the Secretary of State for Wales*,
    York, NCC.

Early Years Curriculum Group (EYGC)(1989)*Early Childhood Education. The Early Years Curriculum and the National Curriculum*,
    Stoke-on-Trent, Trentham Books.

Early Years Curriculum Group (EYGC)(1992)*First Things First. Educating Young Children, A Guide for Parents and Governors*,
    Oldham, Madeleine Lindley.

Fanthorpe, U.E. (1992) *Heck-Verse*, 'Half-past Two', pp.31/32,
    Calstock, Peterloo Poets.

Hartley, D. (1993) *Understanding the Nursery School,* London, Cassell.

Heath, S.B. (1983) *Ways with Words. Language, life and work in communities and classrooms,* Cambridge University Press.

Holmes, G. (1977) *The Idiot Teacher,* Nottingham, Spokesman.

Kelly, G.A.(1963) *A Theory of Personality,* New York, Norton.

National Curriculum Council (NCC) (1993) *Spiritual and Moral Development - A Discussion Paper,* York, NCC.

Nelson, K. (1989) *Narratives from the Crib,* Cambridge, Mass., Harvard University Press.

Schweinhart, L.J. and Weikart, D.P.(1993) *A Summary of Significant Benefits: The High/Scope Perry Preschool Study through age 27,* Ypsilanti, Michigan, High/Scope.

Smith, F.(1988) *Joining the Literacy Club,* London, Heinemann.

Weir, R.H. (1962) *Language in the Crib,* The Hague, Mouton.

Wells, C.G. (1987) *The Meaning Makers. Children Learning Language and Using Language to Learn,* London, Hodder & Stoughton.

Whitehead, M.R. (1992) "Assessment at Key Stage 1: Core Subjects and the Developmental Curriculum", in G.M.Blenkin & A.V. Kelly (Eds). *Assessment in Early Childhood Education,* London, Paul Chapman.

Williams, R. (1961) *The Long Revolution,* Harmondsworth, Penguin.

Four year olds in school: cause for concern

by Jenefer Joseph

Let's start with a few facts:
a) Over 347,000 children in England and Wales, aged four at 31st August, 1991 were admitted to infant classes in maintained primary schools, in the autumn term of the 1991/92 school year. All of them were below compulsory school age and nearly half (170,000) were admitted **more than a term before they reached compulsory school age.**
b) In addition 119,000 children aged four at the end of December were admitted to infant classes in January 1992 - a **term or more before they reached compulsory school age.**
c) Between 1983 and 1992, the number of pupils below compulsory school age in infant classes rose consistently every year - a rise of 43% since 1983.
d) **Over 90% of four-year-olds in infant schools attend full time.**
e) In addition in January 1992 there were 45,900 such pupils in independent schools in England - a rise of 56% since 1983 (DFE 1993).

Thus of all three and four year olds in England having some educational provision, **a minimum of 78% are in infant classes.**

Based on this, it is reasonable to say that four is now the unofficially acknowledged and accepted age at which children start formal schooling in England and Wales. This makes us unenviably unique in the world, five, six and even seven being the norm in all other countries.

How has this reprehensible situation come about? Historically, in spite of the pioneering work in nursery education started by the McMillan sisters at the turn of the century, there has never been a real commitment to the promotion of early years education by any government, whatever its colour. There have been many promises, normally trotted out in election run-ups, but time after time, opportunities have been missed (or rather avoided), and our meagre State nursery schooling has largely slipped in through the back door whilst nobody was quite watching.

The Government White Paper of 1972 aimed to provide nursery education for all three and four-year-olds whose parents wanted it. This too, became a promise unfulfilled, and soon after, nursery classes attached to primary schools began to proliferate, and to act as substitutes for traditional nursery schools. During the whole of the Thatcher years, monetary considerations plus falling rolls were used to encourage LEAs to admit children from four years plus into infant/reception classes.

As to current reasons - some, of course, arise from the historical developments themselves. For example, the continued lack of sufficient nursery provision has made it possible for authorities to claim that four-year-olds are better off in infant classes than having no educational experience at all. The fact that, so often, reception class provision is inappropriate for four-year-olds, is brushed aside in favour of inflating the statistics of under fives provision.

Further grounds include the fact that:
- it clearly costs less to have four-year-olds in a reception class, with a teacher/pupil ratio of, say, 1:30, than to run a nursery class with two staff, where the accepted ratio is closer to 1:15.
- if a school admits children early, it is less likely to lose them to other schools in the neighbourhood.
- there are now more working mothers who, finding no nursery places available, press for their children to be admitted early.

The effects of these various aspects are already considerable, and in order to judge whether they are likely to be beneficial or detrimental to the welfare and educational progress of the children, we start by considering their needs.

The needs of four-year-olds

Whilst one should never generalise about human behaviour, it is fair to say that, especially in young children, there are aspects, such as specific needs, which can be demonstrated to be characteristic of certain stages of development, and which can guide us in providing educational settings which are appropriate for them.

1. **Four-year-olds need space.** They are active beings, and need space to move, run, jump, build, climb. They also need the kind of space which

allows for intimate, cosy areas, where they can enjoy being peaceful and undisturbed.

2. **Four-year-olds need plenty of opportunity for self chosen social interactions** both with their peers and with adults. This socialisation is of the kind which arises naturally during children's activities and which varies and flows from one-to-one encounters to small groups. Young children are trying to understand and cope with the differing social situations which they meet, testing out and clarifying the roles and demands of others, and their own relationship to them. This includes adults as well as children - they need to feel safe and secure in the support of understanding and caring adults and to have the enrichment of experiencing their diverse talents and abilities.

3. **Four-year-olds need time** - to do things in their own way, at their own pace, without being rushed or pressurised. This is an aspect of young children's lives which is often overlooked, especially during routine times, when children are hurriedly prepared for the next event. Children are in learning situations almost all the time at this age, and they need to be able to concentrate for as long as they like, and to remain involved in absorbing pursuits with as little interruption as possible, so that they can complete tasks to their own satisfaction. They also need time for reflection, to think about what they have done, or are going to do, and generally have the opportunities for contemplation which adults themselves seek.

4. **Four-year-olds need to be able to follow their own interests** - to be able to indulge in and concentrate on their own intentions, whether they be creative, social or whatever. They learn in diverse ways, are curious about a great number of things, and they need the freedom, within a secure framework, to explore, investigate and generally pursue what is of significance to them.

5. **Four-year-olds need endless opportunities to enhance their language development,** and their verbal facility in particular. We know that children acquire language largely within the context of the activities and the concerns which are engaging them at the time. We also know that children's language experiences before they go to school vary

enormously, so the linguistic environment, which is provided for them at school, has to be rich, and allow for a great deal of conversational exchanges both in small groups, and in relaxed one-to-one situations, where the adult is doing as much listening as talking.

6. **Above all, four-year-olds need the freedom and encouragement to play.** Central to children's all round development is their need for spontaneous play activities. It is through their play that they make their social adjustments, and learn to cope with their emotions. Moreover, through play children juggle with ideas, *"develop what they know,... dare to take risks, negotiate, solve problems, initiate, anticipate,...reflect on and consolidate their knowledge and understanding."* (EYCG, 1989, p.2)

How, within the Education System, are we to best cater for these needs?

We will examine the three types of provision presently available to four- year- olds.

1. **NURSERY SCHOOLS** are designed and geared to meet these needs and promote the all round development of the four-year-olds.

- They have the **space**, both indoors and out, which gives the children the freedom to pursue their interests actively, and to experience a wide variety of equipment and materials especially appropriate to their needs and capabilities.

- They offer a **timetable** which is both loosely structured and flexible, which is geared for individuals rather than groups, and where the groups are predominantly self-selected, small and random. This encourages children to use their initiative, to achieve independence of thought and to take responsibility for their actions.

- They offer a **curriculum** which encourages children to explore any areas of knowledge which attract and influence them. This, together with the staff ensuring that language, mathematical and scientific development is fostered, gives these young children a broad and sound initiation into the world of knowledge from which they can begin to pursue their individual interests.

- They maintain an **adult/child ratio** of 1:10/12.

- **The staff is specially trained,** having the detailed knowledge of child development needed to understand young children's behaviour, together with the teaching skills and techniques appropriate for such young children.

- **The staff maintain close contact with parents**, welcome them as observers in the school, and encourage them to be actively involved with the children when and where appropriate.

All these factors make it possible for the children to **learn through their play**, the importance of which, in the all round development of young children, has already been emphasised.

2. **NURSERY CLASSES.** Whilst some of these are able to offer much of what the nursery schools do, many have to contend with considerable restrictions on space; often have to modify their timetables to accommodate to the demands of the rest of the primary school; and are likely to have to share outdoor space with the rest of the school. This last means offering dauntingly bare areas of tarmac, bereft of the safety and security that a more intimate and appropriately furnished area gives.

Clearly then, nursery schools and (some) nursery classes provide the educational ambience to meet the needs of the four-year-olds.

3. **RECEPTION CLASSES** differ in various aspects.

a) **Space.**
The class is usually in one room in part of the primary school. There may be a small ante-room, and the corridor may be used in spite of constantly passing traffic. Indoor space, being limited, cannot offer the sorts of facilities available in nursery schools. Outdoor play space is merely part of the whole playground, inhospitably tarmacked and with inappropriate equipment.

b) **Timetabling and curriculum.**
Inevitably, timetabling has to be tighter and more structured. There is a clear division between 'work' and 'play', the latter usually being allowed when the 'serious' work of dealing with the exigencies of the 3Rs has been completed, and children are entitled to indulge themselves in somewhat 'non-serious' play activities, such as creative work, block building and imaginative games. In contrast to nursery provision, the daily programme is dominated by **teacher**

rather than **child** chosen activities, and there is more group work than individual one-to-one interchanges. Moreover, because of the above factors, much important equipment and material is omitted. For example, sand and water, two fundamentally important resources for children's sensory, mathematical, scientific and imaginative development, are seldom available.

c) **Opportunities for play.**
Arising from all this, it is clear that a reception class can offer very limited opportunities for genuinely spontaneous play, and this is profoundly antipathetic to the needs of four-year-olds. As Mari Guha says,

"...to give time for play in school, is not to give a 'break' or rest from learning; it is not a concession to immature minds. Rather it is a way of making teaching and learning more productive........We do not know what the knowledge is, and the skills are, that the children of today will most need in the future. Flexibility, confidence and the ability to think for oneself - these are the attributes one hopes will not let them down. If play is conducive to the development of these, we had better have it in the school."
(1988, p.78-9)

d) **The skills of the teacher.**
We know that a qualified teacher is supposedly capable of teaching any child. We also know that **specialist knowledge** and understanding is crucial for teachers to really succeed with different age groups, and this applies equally to those teaching under fives. Anyone who knows anything about the under eight age group understands that there is a great deal of difference between the skills, knowledge and capabilities of children between four years one month and five years eleven months, the developmental range which can now be found in reception classes. The teacher of four-year-olds, therefore, needs to understand fully how they learn, and be able to cater for it, at the same time as trying to satisfy the equally important needs and demands of the five-year-olds. She has to allow for the children's need for exploratory play; to be able to diagnose and then discuss the children's intentions with them; provide inspired materials at critical moments; help children reflect on their experiences. All these are paramount in promoting and enhancing the children's cognitive progress, and ensuring the quality of their learning. Such highly professional skills emanate primarily from the teacher's sound knowledge and experience of child development at this particular age, and

from her commitment to the notion that children's play is intrinsic to their all-round development.

So, without underestimating the skills, knowledge and professionalism of reception teachers, by and large, they are not as 'au fait' with the four-year-olds as they could be. Moreover, because of the restrictions and pressures which the national system puts upon them, many find themselves unable to educate the children as they would, in fact, prefer. It must be said that many reception teachers do try to offer programmes which are genuinely more appropriate for very young children, but lack of support in the form of resources and staff hinders them. They recognise the stress and fears which 'big school' often brings, and are concerned and worried for the children. Moreover,

> *"Most reception class teachers accept that they have been asked to undertake an impossible task...(and) feel pressured by colleagues and parents to 'get the children on'."* (NCNE 1992, p.3)

Clearly then, it is not the fault of the teachers, but the education system which has encouraged the admittance of fours, at the same time as making less authentic nursery provision available.

It should be added that research evidence into different types of provision for the under fives showed that:

a. Children in LEA nursery schools **scored consistently higher** in tests than children who had other types of pre-school experience.

b. Children with **no** pre-school experience scored lowest on tests.

c. **Most worryingly, the four year olds in reception classes performed at the same levels as with the children who had had NO pre-school experience.**

d. **Children who have attended reception classes as young four-year-olds have no evidence of educational or behavioural advantage over childen who started school after their fifth birthday** (Osborn & Millbank 1987 p.210).

Martin Woodhead (1989 p.2) highlights the folly of the policy of admitting very young four-year-olds to school:

> "...the equivalent might be if some universities proposed to admit young people from the age of 14, rather than 18."

The effects on parents and nursery schools.

The advent of both the National Curriculum and the early admission of four-year-olds has made parents uneasy and anxious about their children's schooling at this crucial first stage. Whilst many appear clearly satisfied with what their children are gaining from the nursery school, they are also concerned that their children's chances of success in the Attainment Tests at seven might be jeopardised if they don't enter the reception class as young fours. They are also under pressure from primary schools who offer early places, and worry that non-acceptance might hinder their child's future progress. As a result, many parents succumb to these influences and remove their children too soon for them to have gained the full educational benefits of the nursery school. This, in turn, adversely affects the balance between the three and four-year-olds in the nursery schools. The three-year-olds are denied the role models of the fours and:

> "The four-year-olds lose the opportunity to be the oldest most responsible members of the group. In the reception class they become 'babies' again, which is particularly undermining for summer born children". (NCNE 1993)

Moreover, it is difficult for nursery school staff to keep satisfactory records on children who are with them for much less than three terms.

Furthermore, the specialist training facilities, which nursery schools offer to nursery nurse and teacher students-in-training, are diminished when there are too few four-year-olds in the school to demonstrate the true qualities of a distinctive nursery school programme. Not least of all,

> "The professional reward for nursery staff has been seriously undermined by the removal of four year olds... Their skills are not used to the full (and they) feel that they have been devalued." (NCNE 1993)

What is to be done about this sorry state of affairs?

People working in Early Years Education have, in the past, been notoriously reticent about actively opposing State edicts which they have considered to be detrimental to the education and welfare of young children. This is partly because the importance of early childhood has never really been acknowledged and has been resolutely undervalued, and so working with young children has always had a somewhat low status. This in turn revolves around the fact that early education has been almost entirely undertaken by women. One can't explore the historical and sociological reasons for this here. But the two factors combined have helped to undermine any resolve to resist, with any degree of assertiveness, Government policies which the profession believed was not in the best interests of the child.

It is this attitude which must be overcome. Until the Government is made to understand that these policies are bad for children, and that teachers have strong arguments that justify such a claim, Ministers of State will continue to bring about situations which are politically expedient but educationally retrograde.

The recent clashes between the teachers and the Government over testing are an indication that the profession is sick and tired of the proliferation of rules and regulations with which they have had to contend since the Education Reform Act. These confrontations are already encouraging nursery and primary school teachers to make vociferous and country wide objections to another new proposal to create *"A one year course for parents and other mature students.....who wish to train to teach nursery and infant pupils only"* (DFE 1993, p.12) (A further indication of the lack of understanding of the considerable teaching skills required for Early Years education).

One hopes that all those working in the Early Years will be further provoked to join together in force to persuade the powers that be:

- To reverse their ill-conceived decision to allow four-year-olds into reception classes.

- To increase financial and other help to nursery schools and classes so that they can become even more viable alternatives to having 4-year-olds in reception classes.

- To ensure that reception classes which already have four-year-olds in them, are made to conform to DFE guidelines for **nursery** provision with regard to curriculum and specialist staff suited to nursery children.

- To ensure that parents are not subjected to pressures from any source to send their children to primary school before they feel it right for the children to do so.

Persuading the Authorities to take action means taking action ourselves. It means writing, organising meetings, rallying parents and the media, lobbying MPs and Councillors - generally demonstrating strong and justifiable objections. There is clear evidence that the only occasions on which Governmental or local schemes have been reversed have been those when a huge public outcry has forced the issue. Early Childhood educators "need to be articulate, organised and skilful in acting as a voice for young children....They need to become political advocates on behalf of young children" (Pascal, 1992).

.Erich Fromm said *"People today are yearning for human beings who have wisdom and convictions and the courage to act according to their convictions" (1978).*

Those human beings could be the educators of our vulnerable young children.

REFERENCES:

DES (1993) *The Initial Training of Primary School Teachers*
Draft Circular, London, DFE.

DFE   Statistical Bulletin   No.11/93.

Early Years Curriculum Group (EYCG) (1989)   *Early Childhood Education, The Early Years Curriculum & the National Curriculum.*
Stoke-on-Trent, Trentham Books.

Fromm, Erich (1978) *To Have Or To Be* London, Jonathan Cape.

Guha, M. in Blenkin, G. & Kelly A.V. (1988) *Early Childhood Education*
London, Paul Chapman Publishing.

National Campaign for Nursery Education (1993) *Four Year Olds in Reception Classes.* London, NCNE.

Osborn, A.F. & Milbank, J.E. (1987) *The Effects of Early Education* Oxford, Clarendon Press.

Pascal, C. (1992) *Advocacy, Quality & The Education of The Young Child* Inaugural Professorial Lecture, Worcester College of Higher Education..

Woodhead, M. (1989) "School Starts At Five...Or Four Years Old?" *J.of Ed. Policy,* Vol.4, No.1, p.2.

The professional identity of early years teachers: challenges and constraints

by Iram Siraj-Blatchford

This chapter will explore the contexts within which early years teachers work and the essential skills, attitudes and knowledge upon which a strong and confident professional identity has been built. The professional status of these teachers is now being undermined. I will identify and report on a number of government reforms and on some key research initiatives, which emphasize and are concerned with (national) curriculum continuity and progression. I will argue that these reforms and research present significant challenges to the pre-school and infant school teacher in terms of her current and future professional identity.

Early years teachers in diverse settings

Early years teachers can be found in a range of work settings, but clearly the vast majority are employed in infant classes. Others work in nursery classes, day nurseries or combined nursery centres where they operate on a multi-professional basis with colleagues from the social services, the health service and parents. This allows many early years teachers a wider professional identity than that normally associated with school teachers. One consequence of this has been the number of early years (usually voluntary) support, training and professional groups that are active at a local and national level (Sylva, Siraj-Blatchford & Johnson, 1992).

The commonality and experience of working with young children constitutes a special bond and collegiality among early years workers. The individual professional identities of early years teachers are formed within the professional contexts of their work settings and are influenced by the overall prevailing (hegemonic) professional ethos awarded to the occupation. Of those areas of employment traditionally viewed as least powerful in our society, work with very young children, with mothers, work in the care sector, in multi-professional and even in educational contexts, are particularly significant (Moss,1988). These are precisely the dominating features of early years education.

Early years teachers value the experiences children bring with them from home and enjoy building on them. They feel that their professional knowledge about child development and their skills in teaching early literacy and numeracy (and more recently pre-science and science skills) are important. They are aware, more than most, that effective teaching methods and appropriate choice of content must always be based upon their knowledge and experience of children and the way in which children learn (David, Curtis & Siraj-Blatchford, 1992). This includes a strong emphasis on social, emotional and physical development, as children's cognitive development is seen in an holistic context (Cowley, 1991; Bruce, 1987; DES, 1990; Grieve & Hughes, 1990). While many early years teachers may well have resigned themselves to not having a powerful voice, many are also angry about their increasingly 'muted' status.

Early years teachers and professional identity

Most teachers feel that there is intrinsic value in their every-day work and interaction with young children. As Peters (1988) has put it:

> *"behaving professionally means behaving autonomously, rationally and ethically in the exercise of one's knowledge and skills".*

Problems of low morale occur when an individual's professional self-conception is at odds with institutional or wider social perceptions (Evans, 1992). These wider perceptions are often influenced by the media and the products of educational research. In a study of 150 secondary school teachers, Grace (1978) discovered that secondary modern teachers were more vulnerable to such discrepancies than grammar school teachers. Given popular misconceptions regarding the importance of early years education, primary school, infant and pre-school teachers are certain to be even more vulnerable than their secondary counterparts. The key to understanding teacher self conceptions of professionalism is identified by Grace:

> *"a sense of autonomy emerged as being the most prized possession of the British school teacher, the enjoyment of which prevented serious experience of role conflict in this area." (p227, 1978)*

It could be argued that the ill conceived and hasty imposition of a national curriculum and its associated assessment and reporting requirements have denied early years teachers their most prized possession, the very ground upon which their professional identity had been formed, their perceptions of autonomy. Early years teachers have been on the front-line in the process of implementation and yet their concerns, priorities and understandings have been largely ignored.

The work of early years teachers is supported by research and informed by the rigorous study and application of:

- Knowledge and understanding of children's linguistic, cognitive, social, emotional and physical development.

- Curriculum theory, development and evaluation.

- Highly developed observational, interactional and communicative skills.

- Professional ethics and child advocacy.

The practices of early years teachers is based on clearly articulated principles of early childhood education which have been informed by the extensive research on child development and how children learn (Donaldson, 1978; Sylva et al 1980; Grieve & Hughes 1990). Early years educators also recognize the need for continuing professional development. The number of early years professional support groups (voluntary and public sector) to be found around the country, providing inservice training, is testimony to this. However, the large number of groups has led to fragmentation and a 'united voice' has not developed. As a response to this the recent formation of the umbrella body for early years groups, the Early Years Education Forum, has met with popular support from national and local early years groups.

Ebbeck (1990) has argued that early years teachers need continuing professional development, but that there are prerequisites to professional growth. These conditions are becoming increasingly difficult for early years teachers due to changes in the local management of schools and the curriculum and assessment requirements. Ebbeck argues for:

- Job security.

- A reasonable measure of continuity and stability in their work situation.

- Support from their employing body.

- A reasonable degree of autonomy in carrying out their work.

- Adequate time to do their job competently (Ebbeck, 1990).

Important evidence stems from research involving early years teachers in schools, conducted by Campbell, Evans, Neill, and Packwood, (1992). The research identified some of the changes in the nature of infant teaching brought about by the introduction of the Education Reform Act. These changes were characterised by an increase in the number of hours worked, a decrease in the proportion of time spent with pupils and in a wider variation in individual teacher commitment or alleged 'conscientiousness'. Teachers were generally found to be under intense pressure and the research reported:

> *"a universal perception amongst teachers that workloads overall were unreasonable and unmanageable even for experienced teachers; and that there was not enough time in the school day to meet all the expectations currently laid upon classteachers at Key Stage 1. Teachers experienced the work of teaching as an enervating treadmill of hard work that rarely gave them a sense that they had achieved what they intended to do." (p153)*

Campbell et al (1992) noted that the introduction of subject co-ordination responsibilities, the increasing demands of a hurriedly developed and implemented curriculum and assessment structure, and the need for extra-classroom INSET and interschool meetings have all been demanded without any increase in staffing. Teachers were found to be angry with their LEAs for providing inadequate training or support for the changes that have been introduced. They have also become victims of a widespread paranoia, encouraged by government statements, concerning accountability.

The effect of the *White Paper, Choice and Diversity: a new framework for schools* introduced in July of 1992, was to increase the pressure and demoralisation of teachers, threatening their job security with school closures, inter-school and perhaps eventually inter-classroom competition, and performance related pay. Measures designed to tackle the alleged problems of a handful of 'failing' schools has continued to cause disruption and chaos throughout the whole educational system. The White Paper failed to take significant account of important areas such as nursery education, equal opportunities or the professionalism of teachers. By the omission of these issues teachers received a clear and unequivocal message that they did not matter, that their contribution to the 'system' was insignificant.

Top-down pressures on teachers

A number of government and independent inquiries and initiatives (DES 1989, DES 1990, National Commission on Education) have explored the issue of National Curriculum continuity and progression between the pre-school sector and the infant classroom. Many early years educators have expressed anxiety about the possible effects of 'top down' National Curriculum pressures on teachers and children (V.Hurst 1991, EYCG 1989). Sylva, Siraj-Blatchford and Johnson (1992) show that teachers in this sector are provided with inadequate in-service training and that many feel that some of the most fundamental reasons for their becoming early years educators in pre-school settings are being eroded.

> *"The most cited drawback (in nurseries) was pressure to achieve placed on children as well as teachers, followed by 'lessening emphasis on learning through free 'play' and 'too much paperwork': one respondent said she was so burdened by record keeping that; 'I no longer enjoy the children." (p46, 1992)*

The ongoing struggle of early years educationalists to define national curriculum implementation in their own terms (Sylva, Siraj-Blatchford, Johnson, 1992) provides some grounds for optimism. Nevertheless, in the face of uncertainty regarding government intentions with pre-school provision and training many pre-school teachers are expressing anxiety. The introduction of solely competence based NVQs in child-care and the impending introduction of comparability criteria in a new Europe, where most kindergarten teachers have less training than in the UK, are a very real cause for concern.

Infant teachers have had to bear the brunt of the changes to curriculum and assessment since the Education Reform Act (1988). The continued vociferous, and sometimes vitriolic attacks regarding reading standards, educational standards more generally, and on teaching methods and classroom organisation, has left many teachers in this sector feeling defeated and further disempowered.

The overall effect of the imposition of the national curriculum has thus been to replace the ideology of development in terms of both child and curriculum with one of 'delivery'. At the same time, debate on what constitutes 'good practice' has been superceded by a concern with narrowly defined 'effective' practice.

Educational research and reform

In Kenneth Clarke's (then Secretary of State for Education) 1991 December speech he condemned 'child-centred' education and commissioned his 'three wise men' (Robin Alexander, Jim Rose and Chris Woodhead) to bury so called 'progressive education' for good. The discussion document *Curriculum Organisation, and Classroom Practice in Primary Schools* (Alexander et.al., 1992), has since attracted a great deal of critical attention, particularly for its references to Key Stage 1 (see David, Curtis & Siraj-Blatchford). It is relevant to mention, however, that in suggesting that standards of literacy and numeracy have fallen (despite the admittedly contradictory evidence) Alexander et al explain the alleged deterioration by reference to a set of curriculum practices, which they insist have been adopted widely as a response to the 'child-centred' philosophy of the Hadow and Plowden Reports. They claimed that this 'dogma' has been widely used by teachers to support what they consider to be mere:

> *"rhetoric to sustain practice which in visual terms might look attractive and busy but which lacked any serious educational rational." (Alexander et. al., 1992)*

Crucially, as far as teachers are concerned, this 'discussion' document provided no empirical substantiation of this claim. Another influential publication by Alexander (1992) based on the Leeds 'Primary Needs Programme' also argues that teachers classroom practices were overwhelmingly determined by unsubstantiated beliefs or political allegiances rather than practical experience or research evidence.

Alexander mistakenly treats 'discovery learning' synomonously with 'child-centred education' (for example p201, 1992) and early years teachers may well have perceived this contribution as academic arrogance. To assume that the teachers in his study were not convinced by experience or empirical evidence before adopting their methods is unacceptable. The debates surrounding pupil learning, school effectiveness and teaching styles has a long history and any new discussion should be thoroughly informed by the research methods of studies and not just by their findings. The re-analysis of Neville Bennett's research on teaching styles and pupil performance in the 1970's provides a sobering example of the consequences of failing to recognise the need for multi-dimensional analysis of data. The very basis of early years teachers 'intrinsic satisfactions', and their professional standing, is being eroded by pressures to reform education which are designed as solutions to problems, correctly or incorrectly, identified in industry, in higher, secondary or junior school education. It could be suggested that these problems are often exaggerated for the sake of political capital and that the 'solutions' are then foisted uncritically upon the early years of schooling. The irony is that early years curriculum experience may have informed the most progressive and successful developments throughout education prior to the 1988 Act. Despite HMI evidence that these developments had yet to be taken up in the majority of primary classrooms, they have come to be condemned as 'dogma' and the cause of poor standards. The educational principles and those progressive educationalists who promote them have become a scapegoat for governmental failure with its own national reforms. The final cause of low teacher morale could thus be traced directly back to political interference and ideology.

All of this has very important implications beyond the immediate effects upon standards, Campbell et al (1992) point to the deterioration in career aspirations and the implications for the future loss to the leadership of primary schools of experienced early years teachers.

Teacher education reforms

Clearly there are those who consider that it is possible to construct a 'competence' based Initial Teacher Education (ITE) curriculum sensitive enough to promote 'reflective practitioner' models. But early years ITE demands much more than systematic training. Students need to progressively shift their focus from their own teaching to children's learning, they need to find their own professional 'voice' and critically examine teaching strategies from theoretical, moral and political perspectives. It is also essential that we recognise that the determinants of competent teaching are interrelated, highly complex and context dependent.

Perhaps in the early years we have more cause than most to recognise that teaching is a moral as well as a practical and intellectual endeavour. Education in the early years integrates caring and a consideration of the interests of children with a wide range of individual and social needs. As Philip Gammage (1992) has argued the recent emphasis in initial teacher education upon subject knowledge:

> "is so thoroughly tied up with a view of 'delivering' the National Curriculum, that it is hard to see where child-development, sociology, values-clarification, and the wider aspects of curriculum analysis can be included under the exigencies of CATE and the time pressures of a training which, legitimately, includes a large amount of practical application." (p6, 1992)

There are special problems with definitions of professional practice that emphasise competence in terms of knowledge of subject matter and discrete classroom management skills. Unfortunately it is unlikely that Alexander's (1992) research will be the last to lend its implicit support to such characterisations. In the present competitive academic climate research may well become increasingly opportunist and uncritical of hegemonic trends. In considering the accusation that the alleged ideological barriers to 'good practice' originated in teacher education, Alexander claimed that:

> "the heyday of the former training colleges (the 1960's and early 1970's), which coincided with the appearance and maximum influence of the thinking enshrined in the Plowden report, was characterised by a tendency to missionary zeal, some of which persists, especially where early years teaching is concerned." (1992, p200)

We must seriously question the effects of educational reforms that continue to undermine what is now being referred to by Campbell et al (1992) as teachers 'semi-professional status'.

The latest proposed reforms to the training of primary school teachers (DFE, 1993) advocate reduced training to three or even one year courses. This would replace the traditional four year route for early years teachers. This is a major source of concern, especially when internationally the trend is to increase the length of training for early years professionals. Early years teachers are likely to become the lowest stratum of a hierarchical profession. Courses in universities may be threatened, and given the loss of early years higher education provision, the options for teachers to follow higher degrees to advance their knowledge and careers will also diminish.

It is time for researchers and academics to be more rigorous (and perhaps honest) about their theoretical and conceptual frameworks and admit that educational research has a profound effect upon teachers' self identity and performance.

REFERENCES

Alexander, R.J., Rose,J. & Woodhead, C. (1992) *Curriculum Organisation and Classroom Practice in Primary Schools*, London, DES.

Alexander, R.J. (1992) *Policy and Practice in Primary Education*, London, Routledge.

Bruce, T. (1987) *Early Childhood Education*, London, Hodder and Stoughton.

Campbell, R.J., Evans,L., Neill, S & Packwood, A.(1992) 'The Changing Work of Infant Teachers: Some Policy Issues' in *British Journal of Educational Studies* Vol.XXXX No.2 pp149-162.

Cowley, L. (1991) *Young Children in Group Daycare: Guidelines for Good Practice*, London, National Children's Bureau.

David, T., Curtis, A. & Siraj-Blatchford, I.(1992) *Effective Teaching in the Early Years: Fostering Children's Learning in Nurseries and in Infant Classes*, Stoke-on-Trent, Trentham/OMEP.

Department of Education and Science (1989) *The Education of Children Under Five*, London, HMSO.

Department of Education and Science (1990) *Starting with Quality (Rumbold Report)* London, HMSO.

Department of Education and Science (1992) *Choice and Diversity: a New Framework for schools*, London, HMSO.

Department for Education and Science (1993) *The Initial Training of Primary School Teachers*, Draft Circular, London, DFE.

Early Years Curriculum Group (EYCG) (1989) *Early Childhood Education: The Early Years Curriculum and the National Curriculum* Stoke on Trent, Trentham Books.

Ebbeck, M. (1990) 'Professional Development of Early Years Teachers', *Early Child Development and Care*, Vol.58.

Evans, L. (1992) 'Teacher Morale: an Individual Perspective' in *Educational Studies*, Vol.18, No.2, pp161-171.

Gammage, P. (1992) 'Training Teachers for the Early Years', unpublished paper presented at TACTYC Annual Conference.

Grace, G. (1978) *Teachers, Ideology and Control*, London, Routledge.

Grieve, R., Hughes, M. (eds) (1990) *Understanding Children*, Oxford, Basil Blackwell.

Moss, P. (1988) *Childcare and Equality of Opportunity*, London, European Commission.

Peters, D. (1988) in Spodek, B., Saracho, O. & Peters, D. (Eds.) *Professionalism and the Early Childhood Practitioner*, New York Teachers College Press.

Sylva, K., Roy, C., Painter, M. (1980)*Childwatching at Playgroup and Nursery*, London, Grant McIntyre.

Sylva, K., Siraj-Blatchford, I. & Johnson, S. (1992) 'The impact of the U.K. National Curriculum on Pre-School Practice' in *OMEP International Journal of Early Childhood* Vol.24, No. 1, pp41-51.

Early childhood education.......Where are we now?

Rosalind Swann and Philip Gammage

What is meant by 'early years'?

There is no precise definition of the term 'early years'. It is usually used in an educational context; sometimes in a psychological one; rarely in a medical one. In education there is probably enough general agreement to describe the term as referring to those years of education between about three and eight or nine years of age, though, increasingly, there are those who wish to see it as the total period from birth to nine years. This is a position becoming more and more common in the European Community. Whatever one's viewpoint, it certainly tends to encompass (typically) two major organisational stages of educational provision. In its educational context we should note that most countries in the so-called 'developed' world (and even those in the developing world, such as India) underwent a rapid expansion in what has been conventionally called pre-school education between the 1960s and the 1980s: moreover, many of those same countries have tended to see the period of pre-school generally as approximately three to six years and as closely connected with the period of compulsory schooling which has followed. We should note, too, that grade school, elementary school, primary school (the three terms are almost interchangeable) starts in most countries at about six or seven years of age. However, the age at starting school seems to be becoming progressively younger throughout Europe, (Sweden is lowering the age from seven to six years; Holland from six to five; the UK from five to four-plus; and Northern Ireland from five to four). Many educationists have, certainly since the 1950s, and in some cases earlier (Board of Ed, 1931), commonly used the term 'early childhood' or 'early childhood education' to refer to the period of childhood proper, that is well before puberty, which runs from infancy to about nine years or so. Thus, whilst educationists might quarrel about the exact boundaries, there is common acceptance that the early years of education encompass pre-school or kindergarten together with the first three years of compulsory elementary school. Linkage between the two parts of schooling in the early years (sometimes called 'articulation' in North America) is somewhat problematic, however, and certainly not universal. What is almost universal, in terms of policy, is the general acceptance that pre-school or kindergarten is that part of early years, which while desirable, is rarely compulsory; by contrast, elementary or primary education is compulsory. In many western industrial countries, however, it is relatively rare for children to enter elementary school without some experience of pre-school or kindergarten, and research evidence from many quarters now suggests that such experience has good effects socially, emotionally and cognitively, particularly if it is well-planned and appropriately structured. Belgium, Germany, France and the Netherlands have long established traditions whereby almost the total child population will have had such experience (Tietze and Ufermann, 1989). In the United Kingdom there have been wide variations between different regions, because of different policies by Local Education Authorities, which themselves result from a 'mixed market' approach by policy makers in central government. But the average across England and Wales appears to be about 45% attendance at age three, though this is not necessarily full-time.

The roots of kindergarten run deep. The Froebelian term is used widely throughout the world. Many of the great nineteenth century educational theorists did not separate out their ideas as merely being applicable to one narrow age-range or another. Thus the demarcation between kindergarten and elementary school has always been a factor of more organisational than theoretical interest. Many educationists in many countries have been concerned to emphasise the dangers in allowing formal curricula to press down from the elementary school onto the kindergarten; they have been equally concerned to advocate that the transition should be smooth and a developmental perspective the main theoretical guide (Schools Council, 1992; Olmstead and Weikart, 1992). One distinction between the two levels is common; whilst there is an increasing blurring of child care with the educational function at the pre-school level, this is not the usual case with elementary school. In the past some countries, for example the United States of America, have made very clear distinctions between care functions and early education ones. To a lesser extent this has also been true of France. Tietze and Ufermann claim that this distinction is becoming more blurred throughout the developed world (op. cit., 1989).

It should also be noted also that, increasingly, pre-school teachers are being trained alongside primary teachers or in similar courses of similar length and status. But,

> *"With the exception of a few countries entry qualifications and salaries of pre-school teachers are lower than those of their primary school colleagues, which illustrates the somewhat universal belief that the younger the children the less their teachers need to be qualified and paid."*
> (Tietze and Ufermann, 1989, p75; see also Pascal and Bertram, 1993)

Currently (1993) the British Government is in the period of 'deciding' whether shorter training for teachers of the young is feasible and desirable; and a proposal for radically different (and shorter!) courses of training has surfaced. Professional opposition to such proposals is acute, especially at a time when research evidence points very clearly to the relationship between quality training and quality provision.

For the early years of childhood, one can see that, despite two different levels of organisation (and in the past, of training), there is increasing acknowledgement that this period of childhood should be regarded as a smooth continuous period of development, that institutions should be cognizant of this and should not display marked changes in style or presentation of their socialization processes. Though dangerous to over-simplify, it could be said that increasingly there is the tendency for many governments to see the period of the early years more holistically and for them to formulate policy and legislate accordingly. We can see in British Columbia's 'Year 2,000' policy, for instance, a clear indication of a 'seamless' approach to the education of children from about four to nine years of age. (Province of B.C., 1990) In England and Wales there is the marked tendency to include four-year-old provision in existing primary schools; and currently about 78% of children aged about four years and ten months are in such provision. It is not necessarily desirable, but we should remember that in England there was once a long tradition of admitting three-year-olds into elementary education, since this happened quite commonly throughout the latter part of the nineteenth century. In Alberta 'articulation' between early childhood services (ECS ages 3 to 6 years) and elementary school has become provincial policy. In the former Soviet Union such articulation was state policy (though one should bear in mind that compulsory elementary school still does not start until seven years of age in many parts of the former U.S.S.R., despite the (then) 1985 Soviet Education Act which planned to start primary school a year earlier, at six).

It should be emphasised that in most countries different ratios of staff to children are adopted at different stages of educational provision; and, although there is a marked tendency to blur the distinction between the pre-school and primary stages in education of the early years in terms of process and curriculum content, there is considerable variation in the teacher:child ratio. Usually the teacher, or adult provision is more generous for the children of non-statutory school age. One of the common criticisms of the current British policy of admitting four-year-olds into primary schools is that the adult:child ratios are entirely inappropriate.

In all, the early years of childhood are recognised as very varied developmentally, and there is considerable consensus among educators in the western world that a largely ungraded approach should be taken towards educational provision between the ages of about three and, say, nine years of age. The Sullivan Commission (Sullivan, 1988) considered ungraded approaches as desirable until about nine years of age.

The Jesuits appeared to think the malleable and variable early years lasted until about seven. In the end, all decisions are arbitrary and depend upon individual circumstance and specific context. But, given that with normal developmental variation taken into account, a not insignificant minority of children reach puberty at nine to ten years of age, it seems sensible to talk of the early years as encompassing those critical periods of development which lie between the years of the toddler and the nowadays fast maturing nines. We should recall also that children are partly social products, in many respects more in today's society and fashions than are their parents; and often more alert and conditioned by them. Whatever stages of education are encompassed, therefore, we have used that approximate period for our discussion, secure in the knowledge that, for the most part, sensitive and research-aware educational practices are becoming increasingly unified, ungraded and developmentally focussed during those crucial years.

However, continuity and progression are not simply terms increasingly applicable to *systems* of education, they are fundamental to the ways we view children and their learning. Whilst it may be convenient, and indeed a central part of our own adult modes of thinking, to categorise and compartmentalise, learning is genuinely 'seamless'. As John Holt would have said, we are 'learning all the time'. Moreover, the human brain has the capacity to reconnect and transfer ideas across a life time, as well as across the conventional disciplines or frameworks of scholarship. Indeed, without such a capacity, many of the advances in human knowledge, the connections between biology and engineering, between electronics and music, for example, would not have been possible.

For children continuity and progression continue outside school as well as inside. It is sometimes forgotten that some children go from WRITING to READING, not the other way round, that continuity and progression are about making connections in the child's mind, not in simple adult-imposed sequences.

There is little doubt that continuity and progression need to be in-built assumptions to any plans by the teacher. The British HMI talked of ways in which the planning of lessons should be explicit such that progression could be 'secured' (DES, 1991, p13). But such planning requires the careful observation and recording of a good anthropologist. We should not be in the business of simply fitting children into assumed linear progression in domains of knowledge, rather, be certain that we are constantly on the lookout for the most appropriate way of expanding or developing the child's ideas and interests. The old Quaker phrase is perhaps the most apposite lode star to operate by. We should surely try to 'speak to their (the children's) condition'. This means that real continuity and progression is a building on the point where each child is. Furthermore, it is dangerous to assume that, because a child has achieved a certain level of manipulation or of cognitive skill now, that he or she can automatically repeat that process later on. There are skirmishes with ideas, retrenchement, hesitations, confidence, manners of accommodation to other ideas, all of which make continuity a subtle and difficult thing to chart. Ideas are often like ripples in a pond, spreading outwards, altering the dynamic then settling down, stopping when they meet an obstacle and so on. The sensitive teacher treats linear schemes of progression with caution; useful guidelines, but not much more.

What is meant by 'curriculum'?

A curriculum means literally 'a course to be run', from the latin verb currere. Education and the history of childhood are inseparably linked; and one has only to look at the sorts of curricula proposed by our ancestors to see that they often intended such courses to cover every aspect of physical, social, intellectual and moral life of the child. Indeed, as one might expect, the former three were often totally subservient to the over-riding concern with the latter. The 'course to be run' was expected to lead to death, a close enough phenomenon for the vast majority of young children in the days before hygiene and birth-control. But, more importantly, it was a course which led to salvation and to life after death. Thus, many curriculum pronouncements were concerned to prevent frolic, designed to induce soberness and obedience, certainly concerned with humility and often with the nobility of pain. Plato's prescription, 'Let your children's education take the form of play' did not usually find much of a following in the years before Rousseau and the Romantics. For the most part the curriculum could be best summed up as follows:

> *"Habits, in general, may be very early formed in children. An association of ideas is, as it were, the parent of habit. If, then, you can accustom your children to perceive that your will must always prevail over theirs, when they are opposed, the thing is done, and they will submit to it without difficulty or regret. To bring this about, as soon as they begin to shew their inclination by desire or aversion, let single instances be chosen now and then (not too frequently) to contradict them. For example, if a child shews a desire to have any thing in his hand that he sees, or has any thing in his hand with which he is delighted, let the parent take it from him, and when he does so, let no consideration whatever make him restore it at that time."*
> (Witherspoon, quoted in Greven, 1973, p91)

After birth control and Freud, however, attitudes towards children could never be quite the same; and however one regards the determinants of present views of childhood (i.e. out of Rousseau, Froebel and the Romantics came forth the post-Freudian child!), modern views of appropriate curricula for early childhood are unlikely to take such delight in repression as apparently did Witherspoon. Indeed, as has been mentioned earlier, developmentally appropriate educational practice now has a long and well-researched pedigree.

As Lawton has pointed out, not only is the term curriculum itself a metaphor for a particular course to be 'run', it is also a term which is shot through with metaphors describing how it should be done or what elements really deserve emphasis (Lawton, 1984). Consequently, in curriculum discourse it is possible to hear descriptions such as might be more usefully employed in gardening; ideas as 'seed-beds', for instance, or the word 'kindergarten' itself. More formally, in the language of the curriculum theorist one might commonly hear terms like 'core-curriculum', or talk of a curriculum which 'stretches' children, of a developing or 'spiral' curriculum, and so on.

Quite clearly, whatever the language employed, the curriculum, even for the very young, does consist of plans which represent ideas, concepts, developments, progressions, linkings, and so on, which one hopes the children will follow so that they learn about those elements thought to be worthwhile. Fundamental to the design of any curriculum therefore are purposes and aims. Presumably the purpose of schooling and hence the school curriculum is to bring to the children that selected experience and knowledge which adults (by consensus?) think most important for the continuation of that particular culture, country or group. But within that simple statement lies all manner of problems ambiguities and downright conflicts. Who determines what children should learn and in what manner? For a curriculum is about the 'how' of the process, as well as the 'what' of the content. Should it be the parents, the government, the schoolteachers themselves? Should the children have a say in it? Are they 'clients' in any sense? There are more, many more complications too. It would seem important to know when a curriculum has been successful, that is 'appropriately' absorbed or internalised in some way by the children. To know this is in any real detail is a near impossibility, but it means that most writers on curriculum acknowledge that evaluation is an important element in it all. Indeed the generic, or overarching view of the curriculum usually considers three basic elements, *after* the discussion of purposes or intentions. These are:

1. What content and how determined?

2. What processes, or forms of transmission/interaction are to be used?

3. What methods can we use to assess whether the process has been a success?

There are well-worn traditions and arguments concerning the principles by which a curriculum is designed. Briefly, these take versions of the three questions asked above and try to distill or analyse within them an appropriate way forward. At the level of early childhood, a slight variation occurs on them in that teachers will sometimes ask baldly, WHAT should I be doing, WHEN should I be doing it, and HOW? Answers to such questions are not easy, but it is fair to say that most answers consonant with what is known about the normal growth and development of children will talk about *matching* the activities to the cognitive level of the child, or will use a phrase such as, 'taking account of the entering characteristics of the learner'. In particular, the HOW must be through transactions which are active rather than passive and which allow the child to be fully engaged with the chosen materials or ideas.

Many early childhood educators would aver that the principal considerations should be those concerning that cargo of experiences and understandings that the young child brings with her, since these set the scene into which all activities must fit. It could be argued that adults and those more sophisticated than young children can 'put up' with curricula designed *outside* of their interests and concerns, that is curricula which take no account of their 'entering characteristics'. This is far from ideal, but happens quite regularly, especially if those designing the learning experiences think that knowledge is passively received and not interacted with, or altered by individual perception. With young children, who are usually of markedly different levels of experience and conceptual development, it seems imperative that some sort of awareness of, diagnosis of, or familiarity with the child's perspectives should precede the attempts to construct a curriculum.

One hundred years of psychology, not to mention the vast experience of children gathered beforehand, makes it very apparent that, in Piaget's terms, children develop their cognitive awareness in sequences roughly corresponding to sensori-motor awareness, through concrete experience and analogous reasoning, through ever increasing sophistication to those ideas which are entirely abstract (logical, hypothetical-deductive thinking). It is generally accepted that the notion of stages in learning is both slippery (i.e. When does one stage become another?) yet profound; and whilst there is much criticism of the artificiality of stages (as well as of the apparent mistakes made by Piaget in the language employed when conducting experiments on observing reasoning), there is overall agreement that children do pass through such sequences of conceptual development. Awareness of this work, or rather of its implications, has had a profound effect upon those designing early childhood curricula.

The legacy of Piaget, whilst vast and manifest throughout education, is by no means the only one to affect early childhood curricula, however. There are many others whose imprint is particularly noticeable, though often at the level of assumed ideology rather than demonstrable theory. Principal among these is Froebel. He it was who elevated the centrality of play to near mystic proportions, such that for those concerned with the very early years it has dominated much of the thinking about appropriate modes of learning. Anning says,

> "Early years educators have always set a high value on children's ability to learn through play. In part this is a reflection of the importance they ascribe to learning through 'first-hand experiences'." (1991, p29)

The combination of Piagetian views about the desirability of concrete experience during the early stages of conceptual development, coupled with the notions of play and similar 'first-hand' experience have made a heady mix and a pervasive ideology for much that passes as curriculum planning for the first stages of early childhood education. It is not our purpose to discuss the thin research base of such notions.

Those have been dealt with at length by writers such as Smith and Cowie (1991). Suffice it to say that the 'heady mix' referred to earlier is certainly one well ingrained in many western systems of provision. This is so much the case that some might consider talk of a curriculum at the pre-five or six year level to be inappropriate. A curriculum proper, as it were, would be considered more to do with basic skills in literacy and numeracy, and, as such, to be left to the later stages of planning early childhood education.

Developmentally appropriate practice.

Rather than talk of curriculum, some researchers have preferred to use terms such as practice, experience, or programmes, and then discussed these in relation to what they believe to be overarching principles distilled from decades of research in child development. Typical of these would be Elkind (1989), Fishbein (1976), Katz, (1979). In reality there is not much division between the curriculum writers and the programme writers. Both groups, especially the more careful, are at pains to separate ideology and assumption from research and theory wherever it is feasible to do so. But the term 'developmentally appropriate practice' is perhaps especially useful since it keeps the prime feature to be accounted for in the forefront of one's mind. What conceptual levels are these children at?

Elkind writes of three basic principles which he sees as the foundations upon which much early educational practice is based. These are:

1. Multi-age grouping, which he says *"derives from the normal variability among young children"* (1989, p47).

2. Non-graded curricular materials (This means interest areas, games, books, blocks, water and sand, materials which can be used at different scientific levels, such as magnifying glasses, balance scales, magnets, etc) The idea is that these may be used in different ways by different ages and stages of child, such that the activity, level of curiosity, or sophistication of observation fits easily into the conceptual needs of the child.

3. Interactive teaching, *"in which the teacher serves as a matchmaker between child and materials. Effective interactive teaching means that the teacher must have a solid understanding of both the intellectual demands of the materials and the cognitive abilities of the children"* (ibid). Brierley, talking

of intervention at the right time, says that Christian Schiller once wrote of a headmaster who had said,

"I always say to teachers, leave the children alone until they need help: but remember that they won't come and tell you when that moment comes. To seize that moment is the art of teaching young children" (1987,p73). Brierley writes too of the appropriate environment of many nursery and infant schools being ones which inspire **'experiment, imagination and talk'** and of the exploring child 'behaving very much like a scientist'. Elkind reminds one that establishing a developmentally based approach is not easy. Of materials, he says, *"Materials need enough structure to give children guidance, but also enough openness to pose a challenge to their intelligence"* (Elkind, op cit, p51).

Internationally, early childhood educators are in clear agreement over what they see in children. They see children as active operators upon the environment and already actively 'programmed' to learn and absorb those things which interest them. The skilful teacher of four or five-year-olds is not likely to separate cognitive development from those associated motivational, social and affective aspects of that same child's development. At the moment, however, there is some degree of tension between those who see it essential to provide a structured 'outside designed' curriculum (specially prepared to concentrate on the basic skills and those areas of knowledge deemed necessary for the country's good) and those who see the child development perspective as being the essential shaper of the experiences to be put before the young child. Katz maintains that learning take splace in four basic dimensions: learned feelings, knowledge, skills and dispositions, but that these can be damaged by the wrong approaches (Katz, 1987). Again, such a view appears to match similar views and perspectives of other child developmentalists (for example, Elkind, 1987, Bredekamp, 1987). It can sometimes be expressed by the aphorism, *'We are concerned that children should be able to question the answers, not answer the questions'.*

Developmentally appropriate practice may be summed up thus: It is vital that the experiences provided for young children are in line with what we know about their development, about the intense critical periods within those sequences of development, and are in line with a view of the organism as active and exploring. As Morgan has said,

Where are we now?

> *"It is vital for children to use skills actively. Children need to use skills such as talking, matching, classifying and constructing. They do not need so much to be taught these skills, but they do need an environment in which they can be encouraged and assisted to use them. Instead schools may stress listening skills at the expense of talking skills, and skills in memorizing meaningless abstractions without the reality of sensory experience."* (Morgan,1989, p42)

All in all, whether one takes a strictly curricular view and employs the 'theory' embodied in curriculum writings, or whether one takes a consciously less curriculum structured approach, one comes to the same conclusions:

- Start from where the children really are.

- Use careful observations of what they need.

- Ensure that the design of materials and programmes involve detailed knowledge of the children.

- Then, however one describes them, the processes are most likely to capitalise on all that the child has; emotions, thoughts and physical and social skills. In this way the child may advance. As Brierley notes: *"A child remembers only those things to which he pays keen attention. None of the things he ignores appears to leave a memory trace in the brain"* (Brierley 1987, p112).

As the reader will have noted, it is impossible to talk about develomentally-based practice without constant referral to the curriculum as a whole. In reality the two aspects cannot be separated because they are part of the interlocked chain of decisions and processes which go to make up the central work of the school. The National Association for the Education of Young Children (USA) say that:

> *"The early childhood profession defines curriculum in its broadest sense, encompassing prevailing theories, approaches, and models."* (NAEYC, 1991, p21)

In this way questions about **how children best learn** are as important (perhaps MORE important) than questions about what should be learned, or about the way it should be assessed.

Central to much that has been cherished in the developmentally-based practice of early childhood educators has been the notion of grouping children in various ways. This has been a prevailing ideology going back at least to the early part of this century. But sometimes group work is of not much more use intellectually than, say, grouping children by size, or by the colour of their hair! Bennett has pointed out that groups are often no more than,

> *"collections of children sitting together but engaged on individual work. In such groups the level of cooperation, frequency of explanations and knowledge exchange is low."* (Bennett, 1991, p58)

The important thing to note about Bennett's studies is that, by adapting a cautious Piagetian model of the way children's conversations appear to develop, Bennett and his associates **were** able to set up groups where the tasks were explicit, where the task protocols were available to the teachers and where the children were able to talk effectively and cooperate such that the application and achievement were demonstrable. Bennett makes the point that he is **not** prescribing his approach to group work as **the** method:

> *"What I do advocate is a better balance of teaching approach than at present between individual, group and whole class teaching, with grouping perhaps taking a pre-eminent role in problem solving and application tasks."* (Bennett, op cit, pp592-593)

What underlies much of the debate about curricula, or, indeed, aspects of developmentally-based practice, is really the fundamental (but very distracting) content versus process debate. But note that the adherents of a developmental approach to early childhood are rarely, if ever, suggesting that content is not important. If children are to talk purposefully about some things, there have to be those things to select. If they are to write about something, or to solve problems, then those problems have to be available in some form. Thus, inevitably, adults make selections from the knowledge base of the culture itself. The point at issue is that children are not simply miniature repositories of adult culture. If that were the case a sort of intellectual stasis would soon set in. Children construct knowledge; they make errors as they move forward. But, in doing so, they move forward as somewhat different beings from us. In this respect children may be regarded as social constructs in themselves; already more accepting, perhaps more curious, more knowledgeable, perhaps more sophisticated than ourselves. We know that this is the case from countless studies of children's language, both spoken and written. In summary form the NAYC encapsulates the current position neatly in their 'mission statement':

Children **CONSTRUCT** knowledge; children learn through **SOCIAL INTERACTION**; children's learning moves typically through **AWARENESS, EXPLORATION, INQUIRY**, and **UTILISATION;** children learn through **PLAY**; their interests are crucial **MOTIVATORS;** they **VARY** enormously in their capacity and progress (NAYC, 1991 pp26-27).

References

Anning, A. (1991) *The First Years at School*, Milton Keynes, Open Univ. Press.

Bennett, N. (1991) The Emmanuel Miller Memorial Lecture 1990, Cooperation in classrooms: processes and outcomes, *Journal of Child Psychologyand Psychiatry*, vol 32, no 4, pp 581-594.

Board of Education (1931) *The Primary School*, HMSO, London.

Bredekamp, S. ed. (1987) *Developmentally Appropriate Practice in Early ChildhoodPrograms Serving Children from Birth through Age 8*, Washington, DC, National Assoc'n for the Education of Young Children.

Brierley, J. (1987) *Give Me a Child Until He is Seven*, Lewes, East Sussex, Falmer Press.

D.E.S. (1991) *Science: Key Stages 1 and 3*, a report by HMI on the first year, 1989-1990, London, HMSO.

Elkind, D (1989) Developmentally Appropriate Education for 4-Year-Olds, *Theory Into Practice*, vol 28, no 1, pp 47-52.

Fishbein, H D (1976) *Education, Development and Children's Learning*, Pacific Palisades, California, Goodyear.

Katz, L (1979) *Helping Others Learn to Teach*, University of Illinois, ERIC.

Katz, L (1987) Early Education: What should Young Children be Doing?, in Kagan, S.,and Zigler, E. eds. *Early Schooling: The National Debate*, New Haven, CT, Yale University Press.

Lawton, D (1984) Metaphor and the Curriculum, in Taylor, W. ed. *Metaphors of Education*, London, Heinemann.

National Association for the Education of Young Children and National Associationof Early Childhood Specialists, (1991) Guidelines for appropriate curriculum content and assessment in programs serving children age 3 through 8, *Young Children*, March, pp 21-38.

Morgan, G (1989) Stalemate or consensus? Barriers to national policy, *Theory into Practice*, 28, 1, pp 41-46.

Olmstead, P.O. and Weikart, D. P. eds (1992) *How Nations Serve Young Children:Profiles of Child Care and Education in 14 Countries*, Ypsilanti, Mi: High Scope Foundation.

Pascal, C. and Bertram, A.D.(1993) The Education of Young Children and Their Teachers in Europe, *European Early Childhood Education Research Journal*, vol 1, no2, pp 27-38.

Province of British Columbia, (1990) *Year 2000: A Curriculum and Assessment Framework for the Future*, Victoria, B.C. Ministry of Education.

Schools Council, National Board of Employment, Education and Training, (1992) *Developing Flexible Strategies in The Early Years of Schooling: Purposes and Possibilities*, Canberra, Australian Government Publishing Service.

Smith, P.K.and Cowie, H. (1991) *Understanding Children's Development* (second edition) Oxford, Blackwell.

Sullivan, B.M. (1988) *A Legacy for Learners (The Sullivan Commission)* Victoria, B.C. Queen's Printer for British Columbia.

Tietze W. and Ufermann K., (1989) An international perspective on schooling for 4-year-olds, *Theory Into Practice,* 28, 1, pp 69-77.

Witherspoon, J. (1973) Letters on Education, 1797, in Greven, P.J. *Child-Rearing Concepts,* 1628-1861, Itasca, Ill, Peacock Publishers.

Postscript:

Early childhood education : ten points of good practice

Research from many disciplines and gathered over a considerable period of time points clearly towards an education for the young child which (ideally) is:

1. **ACTIVE**: that gives plenty of hands-on involvement, rather than assumes passive receipt by the child.

2. **PERSONALLY MEANINGFUL**: that capitalises clearly on what children are interested in.

3. **EXPERIENTIAL**: that plans for learning by doing, talking, experimenting.

4. **EXPLORATORY**: that invites possibilities, delights in curiosity as a key motivator.

5. **DEVELOPMENTALLY APPROPRIATE**: that is carefully suited to the age and stage of each child.

6. **PRO-SOCIAL**: that provides for appropriate interaction and stresses co-operation rather than competition.

7. **CREATIVE**: that encourages children to be inventive and imaginative.

8. **PROCESS-ORIENTED**: that recognises the need to help children through complex processes in appropriate steps and stages.

9. **INTEGRATED**: that is (as much as possible) holistic and not broken down into meaningless sub-skills.

10. **RIGOROUS**: that stresses child responsibility, initiative and commitment; is conceptually developing and moving towards higher order thought processes.

Notes on contributors

Philip Gammage trained and taught as a primary school teacher in London before eventually studying for a Ph.D in Psychology. After some years training teachers at Furzedown College, he worked at the University of Bristol. He has taught in Australia, Canada, Greece, Malta, Spain, and the USA. He is currently Dean of Education at the University of Nottingham and chairperson of the national organisation for trainers of early years teachers (TACTYC).

Jenefer Joseph was formerly a Senior Lecturer in Early Childhood Education. She has taught as a nursery/infants teacher. She spent a year in Morocco as a Day Care Consultant, and a year in Australia as Visiting Fellow in Early Childhood Education. She has worked for the British Council in India and Cameroon, and has run workshops in USA and Malaysia. She is now an Early Years Consultant.

Janet Meighan was formerly a Senior Lecturer in Early Years Education at the University of Derby. She has taught nursery, infant and primary aged children. A central focus of her research and writing has been the learners' responsibility in their own learning, including working democratically with others. She has contributed to various publications including *The Democratic School* Harber, C. and Meighan, R. (Education Now, 1989), *The School Field* (International Journal of Theory and Reasearch in Education,1990) and has lectured both nationally and internationally on early childhood themes.

Iram Siraj-Blatchford is currently Lecturer in Early Childhood Education at the University of Warwick. She has taught in nursery, infant and primary schools and is co-author of *Effective Teaching in the Early Years: Fostering Children's Learning in Nurseries and Infant Schools* (1992). She has published and lectured nationally and internationally on quality and equality issues the early years. Her most recent book *The Early Years: Laying the Foundations for Racial Equality* (1993) is published by Trentham. Her research interests include teacher education, comparative early childhood education and research methodology.

Rosalind Swann is Lecturer in Early Childhood Education at Cheltenham and Gloucester College of Higher Education. She has taught nursery, infant and primary children in England and North America and has lectured nationally and internationally on aspects of early learning in aesthetics, language and science. She is currently researching the role of early years practitioners. She is an accomplished musician and a Fellow of the Royal Society of Arts.

Marian Whitehead is a Senior Lecturer in Education at Goldsmiths' College, University of London. She has published and researched extensively on language development and early childhood education and is the author of *Language and Literacy in the Early Years,* (Paul Chapman, 1990). Her main teaching responsibilities are for M.A. work in both language and literature in education and early childhood education; her current research is part of a project investigating notions of 'quality' in the training of early years practitioners in England and Wales.

BOOKS BY EDUCATION NOW

Learning All the Time by John Holt £6-50
...*quintessential Holt; readable, accessible, kindly, immensely observant...*
Professor Philip Gammage

Flexischooling by Roland Meighan £6-00
...*a great pearl in his writings*.....Professor Aleksander Nalaskowski

Never Too Late by John Holt £10-00
I applaud this book heartily....Sir Yehudi Menuhin

Anatomy of Choice in Education by Roland Meighan and Philip Toogood £10-00
...*precisely what is needed to clear up present confusion and set coherent, purposeful, productive patterns for the future*... Dr.James Hemming

Learner-managed Learning edited by Paul Ginnis £5-00
..*learners really start to explore and exercise their potential only as they take charge of their lives.*.

Democratic Learning and Learning Democracy by Clive Harber £5-00
Democracy is the worst system of organisation - except for all the others!
Winston Churchill

Learning From Home-based Education edited by Roland Meighan £5-00
...*the rich diversity of the home-based phenomenon is demonstrated..*

Issues in Green Education by Damian Randle £5-00
..*it certainly succeeds in provoking thought*...Chris Hartnett

Sharing Power in Schools: Raising Standards by Bernard Trafford £5-00
...*our students are becoming more effective, self-confident and imaginative learners and workers. examination results are improving...*

Education Now is a non-profit research, writing and publishing group devoted to developing more flexible forms of education within the range of human-scale contexts including home-based education, small schooling, mini-schooling, and flexischooling.

Education Now, 113 Arundel Drive, Bramcote Hills, Nottingham NG9 3FQ

Theory and Practice of Regressive Education

by Roland Meighan

In the UK and the USA, there has been a sustained attack, for about twenty years, on something labelled 'progressive education'. The attack was, at first, tentative, then more confident, and then strident. In the 1988 Education Act and the various subsequent revisions, the attackers claimed victory. Yet the obscurity of the target makes the claim difficult to evaluate. There are two immediate problems. The first is what is meant by progressive education, and the second, what is the nature of what is supposed to replace that is so superior. The opposite of progressive is regressive. **So the mystery investigated in this book is what is the nature of regressive education.**

The books shows how regressive schooling favours:
- tightly controlled learning rather than eclectic and spontaneous enquiry,
- a set curriculum imposed by adults is preferable to a self-directed curriculum
- the view that 'Life is no picnic, so school should be no picnic' so be fatalistic and endure it by getting toughened up.
- teaching being defined as formal instruction and authoritarian control
- the idea that learning to work without pleasure in school is a necessary prerequisite to coping with the pain, frustration and dullness of employment - that is if you get any.

One feature of the return of more regressive schooling has been the emphasis on subjects and the imposition of these on younger and younger children. Yet subjects have only a modest part to play in the scheme of things: they are only part, and a diminishing part at best, of the tool kit of knowledge.

The conclusion is that the switch to regressive ideas in any schooling system is no more than an attempt to refine ancient machinery to try to make it more efficient in the pursuit of obsolete goals.

Professor Roland Meighan ...."has been studying and writing about new developments at the sharp end of innovation for a long time." (Damian Randle)
With contributions by: **Professor Sir Hermann Bondi, Martin Coles, and Professor Philip Gammage and Janet Meighan**
ISBN 0 9518022 3 2   Price £6.00

From:. **Educational Heretics Press, 113 Arundel Drive, Bramcote Hills, Nottingham NG9 3FQ**

Learning All the Time

by John Holt

John Holt's last book 'Learning All the Time', published after his death, focuses on the learning of young children. Learning, to him, means *"making more sense of the world around us, and being able to do more things in it."* John Holt believes young children to be 'natural learners', explorers, research scientists, busily gathering information and making meaning out of the world. Much of their learning, in his view, is not the result of teaching, but rather a constant and universal activity *"as natural as breathing"*. In the book he sets out to show how young children begin to read, write and understand number in the course of everyday life, and how adults can respect and encourage this process.

* * * * *

The vision John Holt had of a school is contained in these words:

"Why not then make schools into places in which children would be allowed, encouraged, and (if and when they asked) helped to explore and make sense of the world around them... in the ways that most interested them?"

* * * * *

John Holt (1923-85) established himself as a writer, educator, and lecturer of significance with the publication of his first book *How Children Fail*. He wrote ten books including other world best sellers such as *How Children Learn* and *The Underachieving School*. His work as been translated into fourteen languages.

ISBN 1-871526-04-3

Price £6.50

Education Now, 113 Arundel Drive, Bramcote Hills, Nottingham NG9 3FQ